FROM TEXT TO TEACHING

A GUIDE TO PREPARING BIBLE TALKS

DAVID JACKMAN

FOREWORD BY DAVID HELM

SYDNEY · YOUNGSTOWN

From Text to Teaching
© David Jackman 2021

All rights reserved. Except as may be permitted by the Copyright Act, no part of this publication may be reproduced in any form or by any means without prior permission from the publisher. Please direct all copyright enquiries and permission requests to the publisher.

Matthias Media
(St Matthias Press Ltd ACN 067 558 365)
Email: info@matthiasmedia.com.au
Internet: www.matthiasmedia.com.au
Please visit our website for current postal and telephone contact information.

Matthias Media (USA)
Email: sales@matthiasmedia.com
Internet: www.matthiasmedia.com
Please visit our website for current postal and telephone contact information.

Scripture quotations are from the Holy Bible, English Standard Version® (ESV®), copyright © 2001 by Crossway, a publishing ministry of Good News Publishers. Used by permission. All rights reserved.

ISBN 978 1 875245 82 6

Cover design and typesetting by Lankshear Design.

FOREWORD

If this short book achieves its aim, you will be better off for having read it. And not only you, but others also—every person on the receiving end of a talk you give or a discussion you lead from the Bible. The goal of this book, then, is connected to the growth and development of people—both your own progress, and that of those who will come under the sound of your voice. And in this I rejoice, for it is nice to read a book that is genuinely concerned with the spiritual welfare of men and women. We have quite enough books already in which the real aim (even if subconscious) emerges from the author's need to blindly impart a set of principles they deem most important. Three cheers, then, for *From Text to Teaching*, because it genuinely has the spiritual betterment of God's people in view.

I can say all this because of what I know of the author. I have known David Jackman (and his wife, Heather) for more than a quarter of a century. David genuinely loves people. In fact, he has in all kindness given his life to helping establish godly men and women. He has done so cheerfully, sometimes in small, out-of-the-way places, gladly enduring long journeys away from home and across the globe. For decades, David has humbly helped thousands of men and women who span every age and season of life. As a pastor, he has loved them. As a preacher, he has shepherded them. And as a prized trainer of young would-be pastors and Bible teachers, he has invited them into his home and not merely into his study. David's material is the stuff of sterling, and his life is the stuff of gold.

One of the things I admire most about David's handling of the Bible is just how reproducible it all becomes for us. What he says and does are things that we, too, can learn to say and do in our own Bible teaching. And so, while it would be a joy to commend to you anything David decided to put into writing, it is a special joy to commend this book. For its author knows that God's people will be loved best by those who are constantly growing in their ability to handle God's word. Put simply, David is aware (as he has reminded us many times) that the word of God must be the engine room if God's people are to lovingly give themselves to Christ's mission.

Having said a word on both aim and author, it only remains for me to touch briefly on the book's argument. Between its covers you will find a beginning sketch—a pencil drawing, as it were—and not a full-blown treatise on everything you need in order to say something worthwhile from the Bible. And yet you will find its brevity one of the greatest reasons for its success. This brief volume is simply out to get you started and point you in the right direction. The introduction provides some basics, and then the main section, devoted to the process of preparation, gives even the novice a pathway that can be trusted. The roadway put down here is not something new (it is not the brainchild of the author's originality); rather, it is a path that is well-worn and time-tested. By following the signposts, you will be both faithful to God's word, and fruitful with the people who hear your words on God's word.

True to form, David provides a very human element in the second part of the book. Here he takes us into his study and allows us to see how he works out the principles in practice. For the beginner, this section of the book will provide a conversation partner, even before you develop your first Bible talks. Beyond that, this short volume goes on to include some of David's valuable maxims on the making of messages. And one can almost hear him saying them aloud even as they now appear here in print.

Well, enough from me. I now happily turn you over to him. For not only will you be better off for it, but so will the people whom God gives you to love.

David Helm
Senior Pastor, Christ Church Chicago
Chairman, The Charles Simeon Trust

CONTENTS

Foreword	i
Introduction	3
The art and science of preaching	5
The process of preparation	15
Putting the principles into practice	45
Using more tools from the toolbox	57
How the text drives the talk	67
Tools from the unashamed workman's toolbox	79
Ten 'commandments' for preaching	83
Appendix: Template for preparing a Bible talk	89

INTRODUCTION

When you see the word 'sermon', what comes to your mind?

Most dictionaries connect 'sermon' with two other words: 'clergyman' and 'pulpit'. And that's probably fair; I'd guess that most people think of a sermon as the talk given in a Sunday church service by the pastor.

Of course, the origin of a word doesn't always tell you much about its current usage, but it suits my purpose to tell you that the word 'sermon' actually comes from a Latin word, *sermo*, which means conversation, discussion, speech, talk or discourse.[1]

So, emboldened by that Latin meaning, I want to claim that this book is about preparing sermons—but sermons of a fairly broad type. That is, I'm not just talking about preaching from a church pulpit. **My goal**

---

1 'sermo', *Wiktionary* website, 2020, accessed 12 January 2020. en.wiktionary.org/wiki/sermo#Latin

is to help you prepare any type of presentation in which a Bible passage is being explained and taught. So, for example, it could be a youth group leader teaching the Bible to a group of teenagers on a Friday night. It might be a speaker opening up the Bible to children on a camp. It might be a woman teaching other women, as in Titus 2. Or, for that matter, it might even be a presentation by a Bible study leader to a group that needs quite a lot of guiding through a passage of Scripture.

Nonetheless, because we tend to be in the habit of thinking of a 'sermon' narrowly as something given in a church gathering, throughout this book I will refer to what I am dealing with as a 'Bible talk' (or sometimes simply a 'talk'). It's not an ideal term. I don't think, for example, it really conveys the seriousness and weightiness of the task in the way the word 'sermon' does. It's not some light and frivolous thing we are doing when we give a Bible talk; it is communicating the very word of God, as revealed in Scripture.

But I can't think of another simple term to use, and rather than spend a chapter of your time debating the pros and cons of various alternatives, let's agree to use the term 'Bible talk' (or 'talk'), knowing that *preparing it* is undoubtedly much more important than deciding *what we call it*.

THE ART AND SCIENCE OF PREACHING

Preaching is both a science and an art.

Science works with certain given materials, by careful observation and experimentation, in order to deepen knowledge and propose hypothetical solutions to existing problems. But it is not a dehumanized mechanical process. The materials, the knowledge and the hypothesis are all in the hands of the scientist. When I remember back to my school days in the chemistry lab, we did experiments in pairs. We all had the same raw materials, the same equipment, the same purpose and the same goals, but some were always much more successful than others in achieving the desired results. The human factors quickly came into play—careful observation, accurate measurements, controlled outcomes—and some of us were much better at doing it than others. Conducting a successful scientific experiment was, in fact, an art form.

At the same time, most accomplished artists will spend at least some time studying the more 'scientific' aspects of their art form. Consider two painters: one has great artistic instincts, and so grabs the nearest set of paints and brushes and begins work immediately; the other has equally great instincts, but takes the time to learn the various qualities of oil-based paints and water-based paints, when to use paint thinner, or the difference between a flat brush, a fan brush and a filbert brush. All other things being equal, which artist is more likely to produce a masterpiece?

Any instruction about preaching needs to recognize both sides—the science and the art of the operation.

There are certain processes the preacher needs to operate, in preparation, which are centred around the careful observation and analysis of the text in question. The preacher has not chosen to write that text; he or she is under its authority, in the sense that all reflection and consequent explanation is dictated by the black marks on the page.

And yet no two preachers will deal with the text in exactly the same way. There is a creativity involved in constructing a persuasive Bible talk, which includes the art of choosing the right words, constructing the most engaging and persuasive argument and presentation, and varying the pitch and pace of the talk to maintain and heighten interest. Preaching is not an art form in the way that a painting or a poem might be, but it is an art nonetheless, and no two of us will do it in exactly the same way.

Does this mean, then, that we need to look for the most charismatic personality to let loose on the congregation his or her 'art' of communication? I think not!

But in order to justify that position, we need to track back to the roots of the purpose of preaching and its role in the contemporary church.

Expository preaching

The sort of preaching I want us to consider is usually called 'expository'. Of course, there are plenty of pulpits around the world where expository preaching (which I'll define below) is not the norm; rather, the approach is to describe a Christian perspective or make a Christian comment or two on the issues that are currently uppermost in the prevailing culture. The focus will be political, or social, perhaps philosophical or speculative. The value depends largely on the quality of the preacher's mental ability and the attractiveness of the presentation. This is the art of the weekly religious commentator, submitting his piece, with its latest notions. It lasts for a few minutes and changes virtually nothing.

But my hope is that you are reading this book because you have a much higher view of the value and significance of preaching than that. Almost the last recorded words we have of the great apostle Paul, to Timothy, his young protégé, is the charge to "preach the word" (2 Tim 4:2). This highlights for us a concern that runs throughout the apostolic ministry and which threads itself all the way through both the Old and New Testaments: that the Scriptures are the written expression of the mind of God; that they are his living and abiding word (see 1 Pet 1:23) given through human channels, but with infallible authority and relevance to the whole human race, in every period of our history. It is this conviction that animates the expository preacher. When the Bible is properly preached, the listeners hear the authentic voice of God. This is not because the preacher's word carries authority in itself, however scholarly, brilliant or engaging the Bible talk may be. Rather, it is because the preacher is captive to the biblical text and recognizes that faithful exposition of the message of the text is the primary responsibility.

Everything hinges, of course, on what it means to preach the Bible 'properly', and that is what we need to explore together in the pages that follow.

Defining characteristics

It is difficult but important to define expository preaching.[2] It is still common to think that if a preacher picks up a Bible, reads some verses, then uses something in

---

2 I have written an extended defence of expository preaching elsewhere: D Jackman, *Why Expository Preaching?*, Christian Focus Publications, 2019.

them as a launch pad, that is expository preaching. It is not. Expository preaching takes the Bible much more seriously than that. Preachers may claim that they have a 'Bible-based' ministry, but often the Bible is merely a springboard from which they bounce off into all kinds of ideas that cannot be justified from that Bible text in any way.

Let me encourage you, instead, to aim for a genuinely biblical ministry, not just preaching that is loosely 'Bible-based'. Our goal should be to emulate the great Puritan pastor John Bunyan, of whom it was said that his blood was bibline—that if you cut him, the Bible would flow out of his veins.

Let me suggest three important characteristics of expository preaching. We shall explore each of these in more detail a little later on, but for now we need to recognize them, since they form the parameters of what we are seeking to do as we move from the text to the talk.

First, **expository preaching focuses on the clear explanation of the meaning of the biblical text**.

I have sometimes expressed this as the text being in the driving seat of the Bible talk. The preacher must never consign the word of God to the back seat of the car, from where it is mostly ignored. Nor is it enough to have the Bible sitting in the passenger seat—the preacher hoping he can find his own way and set his own agenda, with the word of God as some kind of road map to be consulted if the preacher gets a bit lost. The Bible must set the agenda and the direction for where the talk is going.

Another way of making the point is to say that the text is king. As the preacher, I am not in a position to change or amend it in any way. I am its prisoner, its loyal servant. My task is to understand and convey the truth, the whole truth, and nothing but the truth of the text being preached. That could be a single verse, or more likely a paragraph, or a story unit, or a prophetic oracle, or even a whole book of the Bible. But whatever the length, the requirement and the process remain the same.

We must always ask: What does this text mean? Please note that we are **not** to ask: What does this text mean *to me*? That removes the focus from God's divinely inspired word and onto the human interpreter, which will inevitably introduce a strong element of subjective preferences. The expositor's role is to understand the text as completely as possible and to convey its objective meaning as faithfully as possible, because "the word of the Lord remains forever" (1 Pet 1:25). Any word that is merely the preacher's may last a few hours, or days, in the memory of the hearers, but "Forever, O Lord, your word is firmly fixed in the heavens" (Ps 119:89). Jesus made the point even more powerfully when he told his disciples, "Heaven and earth will pass away, but my words will not pass away" (Mark 13:31). Since all Scripture is breathed out by God (2 Tim 3:16), our task is firstly to draw out the meaning of the text, so that its message can be faithfully and accurately conveyed to our hearers.

The second characteristic of expository preaching is that it **sets the text in its context**.

It is often said that a text out of context is a pretext for a proof text, and that is undoubtedly the case. No passage of Scripture has dropped out of heaven as an isolated unit; every passage is situated within a book. What goes before it and what follows both have an impact on our understanding of its purpose. Moreover, no one book of the Bible is separate from the other 65 books. Being the product of its one divine author, the Bible is one book, with one overarching, big-picture story from Genesis to Revelation. Every book has its own particular message and distinctive purpose in the context of the whole Bible, and it is vital that the preacher discovers the purpose of the text under study within the whole-book context.

That can best be achieved by continually asking the question "Why?" Why is *this* passage in *this* place in *this* book? We want to set the text in its immediate literary context, in its historical whole-book context, and in its theological whole-Bible context. This enables us to look more deeply, not just at the meaning, but also at the *significance* of the text. God has set every passage of Scripture in its context for his specific purpose, and we are called to discover that purpose and work with it.

Paul exhorted Timothy, "Do your best to present

yourself to God as one approved, a worker who has no need to be ashamed, rightly handling the word of truth" (2 Tim 2:15). That is the challenge to every preacher. Our task is not only to work hard in order to state the meaning or message of the passage, but also to explain *why* the passage has that meaning and significance. We will only be able to do that when we ourselves are clear about its intended purpose from the context of the book and, indeed, the whole Bible.

This leads us to the third characteristic of expository preaching, which is to **build the bridge from the text in its original context into the minds and hearts of its contemporary hearers, so that its intended effect may be experienced in our lives today**.

This is sometimes called the *pastoral purpose* of the text, or, perhaps better, the *transformational intention*, and it is essential for the application of our preaching to be aligned with God's inspired revelation.

A skilled woodcarver will observe how his raw material is constructed and then be careful to work with the grain of the wood, not against it. For the preacher, the same careful observation and diligence are of prime importance. It is not a matter of thinking up the application, or dragging from the reservoir of our frustrations some tenuous connections with the text, enabling us to 'have a go' at a problem in the congregation. Our listeners will soon learn to switch off when the 'application' comes from the preacher's obsessions, rather than from the significance of the passage. Our task is to convey the intended application of the text to accomplish its intended purpose in our lives, as we respond to its unchanging truth.

Now that we've defined expository preaching and thought about our task as preachers, it's time to start thinking about a process we can follow in our preparation.

THE PROCESS OF PREPARATION

Begin and end with prayer

At this point, we need to consider the all-important place of prayer in the preparation process. In a practical handbook like this, prayer can easily be assumed but then overlooked and effectively sidelined as we concentrate on our own activity. But the balance between prayer and our own hard work is not primarily an issue about the length of time, but about the degree of dependence.

At its most basic level, I see the preparation process as a continuing dialogue between the author of Scripture, God, and me as its proclaimer. My end of the conversation is my response, all the way through, to what I discover the Lord is saying from his word in the passage I am currently studying.

Naturally, I begin with prayer, asking God to open my eyes to see and understand his wondrous self-revelation in his word (Ps 119:18). Because "all Scripture is breathed out by God", I have the enormous privilege of asking the author himself, God the Holy Spirit, to enable my mind to understand, my heart to embrace, and my will to obey all that he intended by inspiring this passage. As the old prayer puts it, I must ask God to grant that I may so "read, mark, learn and inwardly digest" the Scriptures that I may be strengthened by them to live under their instruction. It is important to begin each session of my preparation by affirming how dependent I am on the Spirit's illumination and asking him to minister his word to my own heart first. I must keep remembering that I believe in the Holy Spirit, since it is in his hands that his word accomplishes his work.

From there, the preparation process is one of brief but frequent petitions to the Lord—to understand this difficult sentence, to show me how different ideas actually connect to each other, to help me work out the transformational intention of what I am studying, to refresh me and renew my spiritual energies as I struggle to construct my outline for the talk, or to think how to express my main points as engagingly and persuasively as possible. And so it goes on—here a moment of thanksgiving or praise, there a confession of my weakness and failure, everywhere a deeply felt need for divine enlightenment and help. Whether involved in exegesis, exposition or the brain-aching work of structure and strategy, the emphasis remains the same: pray, pray, and pray.

But the praying doesn't stop with the preparation. Before you give the talk, pray that God will empower and equip you to preach with clarity and faithfulness. Pray for the people who will be listening to the talk, asking that God will open their minds and soften their hearts. Pray for the aim of your talk to impact your hearers, and pray that as you speak God will give you a clear mind, fluency of speech, and a warm heart towards them, that you may do them good. Pray that "the word of the Lord may speed ahead and be honoured" (2 Thess 3:1).

And then, after you have given the talk, pray some more! Thank God for the privilege of preaching and for his faithfulness in upholding you, and pray for the seed to germinate and produce a harvest. Claim God's promise that his word will not return empty, but that it will accomplish his purpose and succeed in the things for which he sent it (Isa 55:11). And should the Lord grant you some awareness that he has blessed your efforts, be sure to ascribe all the glory to him.

Preparation: First steps

We are now ready to start thinking about our preparation.

I am often asked how long it should take to prepare a Bible talk, to which I reply, "How much time do you have?" In fact, it is not so much the amount of time as the way the time is used that determines how fruitful (or otherwise) the talk turns out to be.

Students at seminary are sometimes told that they should spend 20 to 30 hours on preparation. But their tutors overlook the fact that they are not preparing an essay, with numerous footnotes, much less a research paper. Too much time can be as much a disaster as too little. The preacher may have consulted a great range of commentaries and learned what everyone in the history of the church has thought about their text, but to compress all that into a coherent, engaging talk which actually communicates to the contemporary listener is a massively difficult undertaking. All too often, the hearer becomes buried under an avalanche of information.

Moreover, longer periods of preparation time quickly become unsustainable in the demands of everyday ministry, which are always multiplying. The danger then is to take shortcuts, to stitch together gathered summaries of comment on the text, but not to immerse oneself in the word itself, because we've come to rely too heavily on second-hand sources.

Each preacher needs to determine the time they have available for preparation and, if preaching regularly, to develop a pattern or template for study that will become second nature with practice and the passage of time.

My suggestion—and it is only a suggestion, but it works well for me—is to divide your total allocated time for preparation into four roughly equal segments. To do a reasonable job in an expository talk, one probably needs between 8 and 12 hours (some passages, of course, are more demanding than others). In some weeks, demanding pastoral situations or the other demands of life may erode preparation time. But if we divide the time into four blocks, we are looking at between two and three hours per segment. That should be sustainable in a busy ministry life, on a regular basis, provided it is the priority in the preacher's view of their ministry and is reflected in the discipline of their diary.

Another factor to consider is your own attention span. There is no point in sitting at a desk for two hours if you are only working effectively for one hour. It would be better to shorten the length of the study sessions and multiply their number.

Of course, many lay leaders are asked to prepare Bible talks—either for the regular Sunday meeting or for some other gathering—but simply can't fit four study sessions into a single week (because of work and other commitments). In that case, I recommend planning ahead so you can still make time for the full four sessions, perhaps spread out over two or even three weeks. Remember, too, that the less experience you've had, the more preparation time you might need, so it could be wise to allow extra time.

When I was in pastoral ministry, my aim was to set aside about ten hours of preparation time for my

Sunday sermon (usually about 30 minutes in length), which meant 2½ hours or so on each part of the process. We had our church staff meeting on a Monday morning, but from Tuesday to Friday each morning 9am-11.30am was booked into my diary for preparation. My congregation knew that this was my regular pattern, but they also knew that if there was an occasional pastoral emergency during that time, I would of course seek to meet it.

Over the years, I adopted the following pattern:

Day 1	Exegesis of the passage	What does this text mean?
Day 2	Exposition of the passage	What does it signify?
Day 3	Structure and strategy of the talk	How does it apply?
Day 4	Production of talk notes	

The great advantage of this template is that the work can be completed by the end of Friday so that both the Bible talk and the preacher can be rested on Saturday. There is absolutely no need for the preacher to suffer the horrors of Saturday night fever!

The value of preaching through books

Before we explore each of these sections in more detail, there is one important long-term preparation discipline I want to highlight. I am convinced that the consecutive exposition of a Bible book, or section of a longer book, week by week, is by far the best way to feed God's flock. When we follow this pattern, the congregation is being taught the Bible as God himself gave it—in coherent, developed units which we call books, and not in extracts devoid of their contexts.

But in order to do this well, the preacher has to get to know the book as well as possible, so that when it is divided into sections for preaching, the inner cohesion and unity of the material in the whole book is respected and expounded. It took me quite a few years in ministry to recognize what is really quite obvious—namely, that I need to have the whole book, its theme tunes, and its structure in my mind *before* I get down to the business of choosing the length of the preaching passages and then preparing each text in detail. That means familiarizing myself with the book I am planning to preach in the next quarter of the year, now—two or three months before the actual preaching starts. The more my own thinking is marinated in the book as a whole, the more effective the teaching of each of the constituent parts will be. I will have confidence that I am cutting with the grain of the wood, not merely imposing my own thought systems on the text. Today, I would always advise preachers who are planning to preach through a Bible book to start three months before—an hour here, an hour there—to soak themselves in its distinctive message.

Stage 1: Exegesis

Let's begin to work through our template for the preparation process. We begin with the **exegesis** of the passage, which is the work of drawing out the specific, original and intended meaning of the text. By the end of this time, I want to be able to express the meaning of the passage in my own words, to ensure that I have understood it as thoroughly as I can. It is helpful to then sum up its major content in the form of a *theme sentence*, which expresses in a reasonably short space (not a paragraph!) the essential message of the passage. This is what I must preach if I am to be true to the text and its author.

This is not an easy task, but it is supremely worthwhile, and will more than repay the disciplined analysis and thought that must necessarily go into it. Too many talks suffer from "muddle in the middle", as JI Packer called it, because the preacher has not worked hard enough at the central theme.

So, as we settle down to work, praying for the Lord's illumination of his word and that he will enable us to do our own diligent, hard work (see 2 Tim 2:7), the first task is to *read, re-read, and read again*, asking the Holy Spirit to be your teacher. If you have knowledge of biblical languages, use them, of course, but they are not essential for faithful, accurate exposition, as we have so many aids available to us today. If you are able to, read the text in two or more translations. As you note the differences between them, you may be alerted to some of the interpretative issues you will need to explore.

At this stage, I sometimes take a blank sheet of paper, divide it into two columns, and head them as 'Questions' and 'Surprises'. I find this helps me to read with my antennae up, actively looking for what I don't yet understand and for issues around how one part of a sentence or paragraph connects with the next. These two columns provide a helpful agenda for my continuing study.

Depending on the genre in which the passage is written, this investigative adventure will take on slightly different forms. For example, if we are studying a New Testament epistle, the vocabulary, particularly of repeated terms or technical theological words, is an extremely important element to examine. Equally, we need to give attention to sentence structure and to the flow of ideas. Look for those all-important connection words (such as 'and', 'but', 'therefore' and 'so that') and work out how one idea leads into, or modifies, the next one.

If we are studying a narrative, however, it is the progress of the story that leads us to its essential message. What is the problem being raised? What attempts are made to resolve it, and with what degree of success? Where is the turning point in the story, and what is its outcome? In this case, the detailed study of vocabulary and structures may be less significant than the big-picture thinking of the whole incident or the clues in the way the story is told which point to its essential meaning.

A key skill at this stage in the preparation is accurate observation of the text. What does it actually say? The God-breathed text is king, so all good preaching begins with careful listening. And, in this case, we 'listen' with our eyes. We need to give ourselves to the discipline of asking the important questions, which will draw out the meaning. All the time we need to be asking: What is the central meaning and message of the text?

'Why' questions are the best tool. Start with what the author is saying, but move on to questions like why he is saying it in this way, why he is saying it at this point in the section or book, and why this follows or leads to that.

At this point, it is tempting to resort to a sound commentary and let it do the work for us. But I want to encourage you not to do that, because you will never grow as an expository preacher if you let other people do the heavy lifting and then try to assimilate their work second-hand. Every Bible preacher is thankful for the amazing commentary resources we have today, even if their sheer quantity is sometimes overwhelming. But don't go to them too soon. Work with the text, as much as you can, by yourself. Ask God to show you what this text is saying. Keep the commentaries for the difficult sections, when you haven't been able to unravel the knots. Research what the commentators have to offer, or use them to check out whether your interpretation has credibility, but don't lean on them. And don't lean on the recorded Bible talks of other great preachers, either. Be yourself. Develop your own voice. Trust God to use you in your uniqueness, and don't fall for the folly of seeking to be a clone of someone else.

During this first session, the primary questions we are asking are to do with the content of the passage, which in turn means that we must also give attention to questions of context, especially the historical context. It is a fundamental principle of expository preaching that if we are to discover what the Bible text is intended to teach us today, we have to go back to its author and the original hearers to try to establish what it meant to them in their time. What is the setting of the original document, and the reason it was written? The clues to its purpose will all be found either within the text, in the wider context of the book, or in the whole sweep of biblical theology and salvation history. Bible words have Bible meanings, and Bible questions have Bible answers. So although extra-biblical information may be very useful, the essential clues to interpretation are all in the text. This is why it is so crucial that we learn to search the Scriptures. The word itself is sufficient in the hands of its primary author, the Holy Spirit, to lead us into all the truth we need.

Throughout this part of the process, the essential

message of the passage will be coming into sharper focus. There may be several connected ideas, but as we study the structure of the passage, we should be deducing which of these ideas is central and which ideas are supportive or secondary. If we are to avoid the talk being merely an assortment of thoughts, we should begin to work towards discerning the way in which they come together as a unity, and as an expression of the big idea of the passage, which will become our theme sentence. If that is not yet possible, we probably need to go back and ensure that we have really understood the whole text. This is taxing work, but really essential for clarity later on.

My *theme sentence*, then, is the essential content of the passage in summary form and in my own words, not those of another preacher or commentator. It needs to be expressed in contemporary language that my hearers will readily understand, with minimal technical terms or Christian jargon. My ideal would be that if someone who had not heard the talk were to ask one of my hearers afterwards what it was about, they would receive that person's own succinct summary of my theme sentence. If the preacher does not have that clearly thought out and expressed, it is very likely that no-one else will. So when I come to the composition of the theme sentence at the end of the first preparation session, I am already making some of the biggest decisions about the content of the talk.

Stage 2: Exposition

Returning to the task 24 hours later, we now want to move from exegesis to **exposition**—from the *meaning* of the text to its *significance*.

Here, the secret is to keep asking questions about the purpose and intention of the writer. This is an obvious consequence of our doctrine of biblical inspiration, but many preachers fail to dig deeply enough to connect with the writer's aim, as he was himself inspired by the Holy Spirit. No passage of the Bible exists merely to provide the reader with information to be noted or recorded. There is always the intention that the reader will be changed by the text. Even when the purpose might seem to be purely historical, as in many Old Testament narratives, we need to enlarge our limited perspective, to remember that the Jews called these books the 'former prophets' because history is being told from God's viewpoint; they are expositions of God's mind and heart, revealing what happened as expressive of his character and will, because God is the central mover in each of the events, the hero of each story. So, in Romans 15:4, Paul affirms that "whatever was written in former days was written for our instruction, that through endurance and through the encouragement of the Scriptures we might have hope". Exposition has a purpose that goes beyond mere information or doctrinal proposition: to work with the original purpose of the text in order to see lives changed.

This is where detailed work on the context has a vital part to play. In the immediate literary context, the preacher will want to pay close attention to what precedes and follows the chosen passage. We'll be asking these types of questions:

- » How do the ideas fit together?
- » What is the logical connection from 'a' to 'b' to 'c'?
- » Why did those first readers or hearers need to be told these things, and why in this way, and at this point?

But answering these questions will involve consideration of the text in its historical, whole-book context:

- » What is the big-picture thinking of the book (of which this text is one small part)?
- » What is the book's own 'theme tune' or essential message?
- » Why is it here in the Bible, and what is the distinctive contribution of this passage to that whole-book picture?

This is the great advantage of preaching consecutively through a Bible book. We are constantly gaining fresh and deeper insights into its essential purpose and understanding its impact in a variety of situations with deepening implications.

Yet each book is far more than merely an entity on its own. It is also part of the whole sweep of divine revelation from creation to the new creation, to which each part makes its own unique contribution. So this part of the preparation process will be asking how the message of this book fits into, and contributes to, the total revelation of the Scriptures. And that, in turn, will require consideration of how it relates to the Lord Jesus Christ, who is the centre and theme of all the Bible. We preach the Scriptures supremely because we preach Christ.

Recognition of this primary focus will prevent our preaching from becoming merely a discourse on doctrine. Exposition is not giving a theology lecture, impeccable though that theology might be. Rather, it is an explanation of the content of God's revelation, shaped by its focus on *why* this revelation has been given, and always with a view towards transformation of life, in thought, word and deed. Understanding the context will always help us to understand the purpose.

At the end of stage 2, we want to be able to write an *aim sentence* for the talk. This is about more than simply affirming that we intend to convey the truth of the theme sentence accurately and faithfully. The aim sentence should express the authorial intention of the original, since that will be the unchanging purpose of our expository talk on this passage of God's living and enduring word.

Another way of defining the aim sentence is to see it as the answer to the question, "Why am I giving this talk?" or, better, "What am I praying that the Lord will be pleased to do through this talk in the lives of those who hear it?"

In his sovereignty, God will choose to do whatever he wills, and sometimes the results of a talk can be very different from what we expect. People are still being converted through Bible talks they should never be converted through! But, humanly speaking, if we do not have a clear and prayerful aim, we are unlikely to hit the target.

And we have a great promise that should energize our hard work and prayer in preparation: speaking of "my word... that goes out from my mouth", God affirms, to and through Isaiah, "it shall not return to me empty, but it shall accomplish that which I purpose, and shall succeed in the thing for which I sent it" (Isa 55:11). When we discover the divine purpose and appropriate the divine promises in our preparation and preaching, we have constant assurance that our labour will not be in vain.

The theme sentence and aim sentence are not set in concrete. They are simply a summary of the insights we have been given into this passage, at this point. Coming back to them a day or two later, we may well find that we want to sharpen them or refine them, but if we have done the work well we should not need to make any substantial changes.

Stage 3: Structure and strategy

By this stage of our preparation, the talk has a clear shape and purpose, so we can move on to the third stage of the process, which I call **structure and strategy**. Here the central question is how the talk will enable the theme (the content of the passage) to achieve its aim (the purpose of the passage) in the lives of those who hear it. It's here that you'll be developing the outline for your talk, determining how to divide your time between points, and coming up with ideas for your introduction, conclusion and application.

It is during this demanding brain work that many Bible preachers fall down. We tend to prioritize the exegesis and exposition sessions, but then give comparatively little thought to how we are going to get the content across accurately, engagingly and motivationally to our hearers. We tend to hope it will just happen, because 'the word does the work'. Indeed it does; but the work is actually accomplished by human agents, with all our imperfections, without whom there will be no preaching: "How then will they to call on him in whom they have not believed? And how are they to believe in him of whom they have never heard? And how are they to hear without someone preaching?" (Rom 10:14). So, because the stakes are so high, in time and for eternity, we want to fulfil our role as the preaching agents, to the very best of our ability and in the strength of God's enabling Spirit.

For this reason, every talk needs a clear, logical outline. In most cases we are talking to groups of people who come from different backgrounds, with different assumptions and values in life. The larger the group, the greater the diversity is likely to be. Some will have heard hundreds of Bible talks, while for others it may be their very first experience. Either way, we are inviting them to accompany us on a journey. We know its starting point, its intended destination, and the major features of the landscape that we shall visit en route; we know because we have prepared it. But our hearers don't know what the journey will involve or where it will take them. They will value some sort of road map, something by which they can judge their progress and feel as though they have reached their destination. The outline should provide the structure and direction of the journey.

Usually, the passage itself will provide the logical progression for the talk. Go back to the theme sentence and separate out its key ingredients. Check that they accurately represent the main points of the Bible passage, then use them as the main points of the talk.

It is important at this stage not to be seduced by your own imagined cleverness. Sometimes the lure of alliteration or the buzz of 'on-trend' language and ideas can divert you from the primacy of the text. Many a talk has crashed and burned because the alliterative headings didn't really work, or because the expression of the main points became more important than their biblical content. It is not up to the preacher to impose his or her outline on the Bible. That way spells disaster. It leads to the sort of preaching that has its own controlling agenda and then looks for biblical material to support and justify it. Remember, the purpose of the text is not to provide the preacher with a peg on which to hang their hat.

When the main points are provided by and reflective of the Bible text, however, the text itself determines how many points there should be, which will greatly help the preacher to pace the talk. For example, if you are going to preach for 25 minutes and you have three major points, work out how much time you will spend on each. Allowing three minutes for an introduction and another four for your conclusion, you will have 18 minutes left. Perhaps one of the points demands a good deal more explanation than the others because it is more complex, harder to grasp, or needs more contemporary illustration. If that is going to take, say, eight minutes, then you only have ten minutes left for the other two points, and that time needs to be divided in the same way between them, according to how much needs to be said on each.

Don't feel that every talk must have three points, although experience shows that, for the hearers, three points can focus the message well, while also maintaining momentum as the logical line of the talk develops. More than four points is probably too many, but two points can serve very well.

There is, of course, no inherent virtue in length. Preaching for 45 minutes can sound very impressive, especially to a young preacher, but how many of the congregation really lasted the course? In many ways, it is easier to preach a longer talk because the hard choices about what to leave out can be avoided, and the speaker does not have to be so disciplined.

On the other hand, 20 minutes is a good length for many hearers and a great aid to clarity in what is actually said. I would certainly recommend that young preachers begin by working at a 20-minute presentation. It focuses the mind and makes you work really hard at seeing that your talk represents the essential ingredients of the passage.

How to express the main points in an engaging but accurate way is a discipline well worth spending time on. Headings that teach the point in the way they express the point are probably the most memorable. For example, present-tense verbs are especially valuable as they move the teaching directly into the here and now, while abstract nouns and phrases are much less attractive. 'The Necessity of Obedience' in a talk on discipleship is much less engaging and effective as a heading than 'Disciples Need to Obey'. The two present-tense verbs, together with the noun that invites the hearers to identify as disciples, are so much stronger.

While each point should stand on its own, together the points must form a coherent argument, which is the core of the talk. So it is equally important to ask not only "How am I going to express each of my main points?" but also "How can I link them together? What transitions do I want to include, so that the connections become clear to the hearers?" Without clear connections, the main points can seem disconnected, and the journey becomes dislocated and difficult to follow.

Moving from one main point to the next is a 'danger moment' in the talk; if the connection is not made really clear, you will lose people. Over the years, many preachers have benefited from the mnemonic SEA: *State, Explain, Apply*. It remains a good rule of thumb (though, if followed slavishly, it can make an individual's style too predictable).

After we have decided the main points and how they are to be expressed or stated, the next challenge is to determine how we are going to explain their meaning and significance by expounding the text.

This is where the nourishing content of God's word needs to be communicated to the congregation. Don't just state the point and then rush on to illustrations, examples and applications. Feed the people with the content of the Bible under each main heading. Share with them the fruit of your study—in summary form, of course.

This is where the hard work on exegesis pays off, but make sure it is presented straightforwardly, without technical terms, in everyday language. This doesn't mean you should talk down to the hearers; people quite rightly hate it when the preacher adopts a patronizing attitude towards them. But explain what might not otherwise be clear. Invite them to join you on your journey of discovery through the passage, always trying to explain its implications with reference to real-life issues and situations.

As the text is explained, so the application should be increasingly clear. I like to offer application all through the talk, as I am teaching the main points, rather than leaving it all to the end of the talk. For one thing, I can't assume that my hearers will still be with me at the end. For another, my hearers will be much more motivated to understand and accept the main points if I can show their implications for life on the way through.

The key to good application is to spell out what the text's implications for life might look like to our hearers, in this generation. Doing this faithfully displays real confidence in the power of God's unchanging word to change our lives in a changing world.

The big danger here is to move in on the application as the main thing, rather than expounding the text in such a way that its implications become obvious. The former attitude will tend to produce preaching that applies the particular values of the preacher's subculture, bolting on to the text whichever bees are currently buzzing in the preacher's bonnet. This then produces a rules-and-regulations approach to Christian discipleship that can quickly descend into legalism. And legalism kills.

But before it kills, it usually anaesthetizes. The problem with 'bolt-on' applications is that they become so predictable, and eventually so boring, that the hearers develop an automatic switch-off mechanism. When you are hearing yet again, "This means that we should be evangelizing more", or praying more, or reading our Bibles more, or giving more, the general effect is that the preacher is using a stick to beat us into being better Christians.

It doesn't work, partly because it is simply imposed from the preacher's own agenda, rather than being derived directly from the text with all its inherent spiritual vitality and power. What's more, it doesn't address the root issues of the heart, which is where transformation has to begin if it is to be genuine and long-lasting. Instead, it merely seeks to change outward behaviour, under the pressure exerted, for a few minutes, by the preaching.

Let the text teach you its implications in your own life, and then help your hearers to see how a response of faith and obedience will apply to their lives. Transformation of life is always the Bible's aim, but let us seek to encourage it in the Bible's own way.

Illustrations, introductions and conclusions

We have now reached the point where we have settled our *theme sentence*, *aim sentence* and *outline structure* of the talk. Under the major headings (points), we have developed the logical progression of the subpoints, together with the primary applications to be made, as the detail of the text is made clear. Now is a good time in the preparation process to review the timing of each part of the talk and also to consider where illustrations might be needed, since this will usually take up more time in the talk than we are inclined to think.

Most congregations appreciate illustrations, partly because they are often human-interest stories, which we all love, and partly because they offer a breathing space in the talk from the flow of expository information. For the preacher, too, it provides a change of pace.

But while illustrations can be great servants, they can also become tyrannical masters. If the preacher is determined to include this 'great story' come what may, he may well discover that it works against his greater purpose by diverting attention away from the text to a different centre of interest. How often people say that they remember a talk because of the amusing or dramatic illustrations used, but find it hard to remember what they were meant to be illustrating! So we must make sure that, when we illustrate, what we say really illuminates the point that we are seeking to make.

Another positive value of illustration is that it can stimulate practical responses to the teaching of the passage. Your hearers will be especially grateful when you illustrate the application parts of the talk; a suitable story may greatly help them to identify how the passage can impact them personally. At the moment when the preacher has made his application point and then says, "But what will that look like in practice? Let's stop off for a moment and see what it means to...", the motivational level is demonstrably increased. We must never forget that we are preaching to whole people, who have *minds*, *hearts* and *wills*; our prayerful aim should be that, in some way, every talk addresses all three aspects of our hearers' lives.

The *mind* is fed by the explanations of the Bible's truth and the persuasiveness of its logical development, which changes our thinking. The *heart*, the control centre of the person—the inner citadel where we choose our values and make our decisions—also needs to be enlightened and softened, so that what the mind understands, the heart receives and welcomes.

The opposite is fatally easy. Psalm 95:7-8 exhorts us, "Today, if you hear his voice, do not harden your hearts". The most common way for hearts to harden is for us to hear God's word but do nothing about it, so that we gradually build up a hard crust of resistance to its transformational intention. That can be a special peril for us as preachers, too, which is a major reason why we pray for the ministry of the Holy Spirit to soften our own hearts and make us personally responsive to God's truth, so that through our preaching the hearts of our hearers may be similarly affected.

The proof of the softened heart is the obedient *will*. If there is no renewed commitment to living a changed life, in reliance on the power of the Spirit to enable this change, then it is probably an indication of a hardened heart. As the writer of the letter to the Hebrews warns us, "Take care, brothers, lest there be in any of you an evil, unbelieving heart, leading you to fall away from the living God. But exhort one another every day... that none of you may be hardened by the deceitfulness of sin" (Heb 3:12-13). Our part as preachers is to be sure that we have a clear message for mind, heart and will from the text of Scripture, to express this as persuasively as God enables, and to pray that the same Spirit who inspired the word will move in the minds, hearts and wills of those who hear it.

To complete this key phase of presentation, we need to give plenty of time and thought to the introduction and conclusion of our talk. So much can be gained, or lost, in the first and last few minutes.

I think there is great value in coming to the introduction last, because by then you know the main body and conclusion of the talk and so have a clearer idea of what you are introducing and how to present it to your hearers. So let's think first about the conclusion.

The *conclusion* is not an opportunity to re-preach the main ideas of the talk, or to go back and revisit one of the points that you felt you didn't get across in the main body earlier. That way lies disaster. Rather, the conclusion needs to be clear, to have focus, and to motivate the hearer to action. Go back to your aim sentence and use it to stimulate the response that it anticipated. Try to make it as personal and motivational as possible. Don't allow it to be too long or attempt to cover everything; less is more. But do make sure that it has Monday to Saturday in focus; that it answers the question, "How is what I have just heard going to affect my life this week?" Then give time for quiet reflection and resolve, and for private, individual prayer, before publicly leading a brief prayer of response, asking for God's help to put the aim sentence into practice. Invite the hearers to come to you with their questions, uncertainties or doubts afterwards, and encourage everyone to act on what they have heard, perhaps through an appropriate closing song or hymn.

But what about the *introduction*, which is such a crucial ingredient in the talk? Whether you know your hearers very well or whether you are with them for the first time, do not presume on them listening to what you are going to say. That is fatal. The expository Bible talk that begins, "Last week we ended at verse 10 and today we pick up the threads at verse 11" is already gasping for breath! Each talk has its own life and its own distinctive reason for existence, so it has to be introduced warmly to its hearers, who need to be encouraged to give it their attention by being made aware of the benefits being offered them.

It's rather like being presented with a menu in a restaurant (although in this case the choice factor is missing). A good menu seeks to describe and introduce to the reader the various dishes available, with a view to encouraging participation. The same is true for a talk introduction. In effect, it needs to say, "This is what is on offer. If you stay with me on my journey for the next few minutes, these are the benefits you will derive from it."

An introduction shouldn't be too long or complex, but it needs to be arresting and informative. One of the best ways this can happen is by using a contemporary incident or illustration to introduce the main aim of the talk, to which you will be returning at the end in your conclusion. A circular movement of the talk—using the text to prove the proposition outlined in the introduction and then re-emphasizing this point as the conclusion—can provide a very engaging pattern.

So the opening needs to be clear and confident, since it has to involve and enthuse the hearers for what is to follow—a battle that will be won or lost in the first few minutes. If the speaker persuades his hearers that what he has to say will be relevant and helpful to them, the door will open to listen to something far more important and powerful than any human words can produce: the living word of the living God.

Stage 4: Production of talk notes

The final session of our preparation is to **produce the actual talk** in a format that will enable us to present the message accurately and effectively when we stand up to speak.

Writing one's notes is a very personal matter, which means that there are not really 'rights and wrongs' for this last stage of the process; there is only what works for the individual and what does not. Some people can preach well from a few jotted notes on the back of an envelope, but that is because they have done a great deal of thinking, marshalled their ideas, and memorized much of what they want to communicate. A few sketchy notes will not translate into an effective talk without that hard work.

Others are seduced by the idea of preaching without notes, so that they are in constant eye contact with their hearers and, sometimes, so that their hearers will be duly impressed by their tour de force. But unless the preacher has a photographic memory, I have observed that a great deal of energy during the preaching goes into recall of what he or she intends to say. A point is made, repeated, and then repeated again, while the preacher tries to dredge up from the memory bank whatever should come next. It can become very tedious for the hearers and produces a loss of impetus in its effect.

Just as there is no virtue in preaching without notes, so there is no inherent virtue in using a full script— but it does have certain advantages. The chief of these is that it forces you to think clearly about the precise words you will use to convey the talk's content. This should add greatly to the clarity of the finished product. It is easy for a commitment to informality to hide a functional laziness in preparation. When the preacher is no better prepared than to say to himself, "Then I'll say a few words about…" whatever the subject matter is, you can be sure that waffle and imprecision will soon take over. Vague abstractions and woolly thinking do not benefit our hearers, nor do they honour God.

But while a full script can greatly aid clarity, it can become wooden and stilted in its delivery. It is important to remember that preaching is a different skill from essay writing. What is written in the script needs to be verbal, often conversational, in style. Write down exactly what you will say. If the script is word-processed and produced on large-sized paper, it needs to be remembered that taking it in, a line at a time, can mitigate against the flow of the preaching and lead to long periods of head-down reading and loss of personal contact with the listeners.

It is probably a good idea not to script the illustrations, but just to note a memory aid or two to keep you on track. This will vary the pace and intensity within the talk and make it easier for the hearers to follow the more detailed and precise explanations elsewhere in your presentation.

Most preachers probably end up somewhere between these two extremes, with a more or less detailed outline and specific key points highlighted in some detail. But we all have to discover what works best for us. A willingness to experiment, and to critically assess how well the notes worked for us after the talk has been given, will help us to develop an individual approach and style which gradually becomes our own.

PUTTING THE PRINCIPLES INTO PRACTICE

An example: 1 Corinthians 1-4

Whatever the subject, you can learn all sorts of skills and gain all sorts of insights from reading 'how to' textbooks; they can be very valuable. But you reach a different level of learning when you come to put the principles into practice in a real-life situation. As a young boy who was mad keen on cricket, I devoured the 'how to' manuals and developed a good grasp of the theory of the game. But I entered another world entirely when I faced the opposition's 'demon' fast bowler out on the pitch.

So what I want to do now is show how the principles of preaching might work out in practice. I'll do this by taking a section of Scripture, 1 Corinthians 1-4, and working it through with you as I might do on my own in my study. This is not an easy thing to accomplish, since this is all one-way traffic from me to you, so you can't stop me and ask questions. But I will try to anticipate what some of those questions might be and to explain, as fully as I can with limited space, the decisions we need to make and the directions of the text which will determine our travel.

The advantage of taking a section and dividing it into smaller units is that it will give us a better understanding of the crucial issue of context as we seek to rightly handle Scripture (more on this below). We need to remember, however, that every unit of text, no matter its length, has its own unique contribution to the book as a whole. This means that the better we understand the whole book, the better we shall deal with the constituent parts. Ideally, therefore, we should read and re-read the whole letter, and seek to develop a working hypothesis as to what are its major teachings and purpose, before we study a particular section. Of course, we can never do that perfectly, since it is only by detailed study of the text, verse by verse, that our view of the whole is both broadened and sharpened. This explains why so often when we have finished preaching through a book, we feel that now we are really ready to start! This should keep us humble and dependent on the Lord's illumination.

Understanding 1 Corinthians: The 'melodic line'

Having worked in 1 Corinthians over many years, my working hypothesis as to its 'melodic line' or 'theme tune' would be that it is about **the nature of true Christian spirituality as the fruit of the gospel.**

Paul's purpose is clearly to correct and reform the many distorted, erroneous ideas and behaviour patterns that were current in the Corinthian church, especially regarding the aims and priorities of living as a Christian in an unbelieving world. A one-sentence summary might be: *Genuine gospel spirituality consists in cross-shaped (i.e. self-sacrificing) love.* We will need to keep this big picture clearly in our thinking as we use the zoom lens to focus on the detail of individual sections.

Almost all the scholars agree that the first four chapters form a distinct unit in the letter, in which the presenting problems within the church are laid out and the corrective teaching of the apostolic gospel begins to be applied. In chapter 5, Paul clearly begins to turn his attention to the specific moral issues besetting the church, so from the internal evidence of the letter we can be confident that we are justified in treating chapters 1-4 as a unit.

Subsection 1 - 1:1-17

As our first subsection, we shall study chapter 1, verses 1-17. It would be beneficial for you to read this passage carefully now, to read it again (perhaps out loud to assure maximum concentration), and then to read it a third time, ideally in a different translation if you have access to one. The skill we are seeking to develop here is that of observation, which is a crucial part of the exegesis and exposition sections of the preparation process. Most of us today are used to skim reading, just to get the general gist or to look for something that leaps out from the text and attracts our interest. Here we want to do something different: we want to train ourselves to read with our antennae up, looking as intently as possible at all that the text has to say to us. Reading the text several times is an important part of this process.

Begin by seeking to establish, with as much accuracy as possible, what the text is actually saying. But at the same time keep puzzling with the *why* questions, which will take you beneath the surface meaning. For example: Why does Paul use the wording that he does? Why does he say this here? Why does he write about *this* issue?

One of the greatest helps here is when the text pulls us up short and we think, "I wouldn't have said it that way", or "I wouldn't have connected this to that". This type of observation makes us grapple with the contents of the verses and reminds us that the Bible will always challenge our presuppositions and our erroneous thinking.

Do you see how this approach drives us back to the situation in Corinth with the first readers before we begin to think about its continuing relevance to us today?

As we begin to dive deeply into our passage, one of the most striking observations is that every verse in the first ten has a reference to Jesus Christ. Often his full title is used ("our Lord Jesus Christ"; see verses 2, 3, 7, 8, 9, 10), emphasizing every aspect of his majesty, divinity and humanity. But why is this so strongly emphasized at the beginning of the letter? It would be perfectly possible, indeed quite likely, for a preacher to flatten out these verses and come up with three points such as:

1. Christ is the heart of the gospel (vv. 1-6)
2. Christ is the focus of history (vv. 7-8)
3. Christ is the centre of fellowship (vv. 1-2, 9-10)

All that is perfectly correct and gloriously true, but the danger is that many of the hearers will say, "Yes, I know that", and then simply file it away mentally as information to be believed. But is that *why* Paul wrote it? Of course, we don't want to give our hearers novelty for novelty's sake, but if they are not stirred by what we present to them, then it probably means that we have not found our way right back to Corinth yet. We are observing the *what*, but failing to ask *why*. Of course, our preaching will be true doctrinally, but it won't be achieving the deeper purpose of the text.

If all these great statements about "our Lord Jesus Christ" are true, then what is the flow of the argument? *Why* is Paul building up this recognition of the absolute necessity and centrality of our Lord Jesus Christ?

The answer suddenly becomes clear in verse 10 with his appeal "that all of you agree, and that there be no divisions among you". Every one of the Christians in Corinth is on the same ground, totally dependent on Christ for all the blessings of the gospel. This brings the argument to its climax and powerful penetration in verse 13 with the stark question, "Is Christ divided?" That is where the argument is going.

How outrageous the factions and quarrels described in verses 11-12 are now shown to be, in the light of everything in their present Christian experience and their future hope being one hundred percent dependent on Christ. Paul is shaking them awake by asking how they can possibly be divided when they are claiming to be Christians under the lordship of the one Saviour and one Lord and King—the undivided Christ. Paul's simple but devastating logic is that, if Christ is not divided, then why are you? In the light of verses 1-10, the arguments, quarrels and developing factions of verses 11-16 are revealed to be a ridiculous travesty of true gospel spirituality.

Now, of course, we are finding no difficulty in moving from Corinth to today. We don't have to try to *make* the text relevant. The text *is* relevant; the word itself does the work.

What church, denomination or parachurch organization does not find itself beset by internal divisions over human differences and preferences? But if those divisions continue, it indicates that Christ is no longer being given his proper position, even though there may be many things among them (or us) which seem to be commendable and right (see vv. 5-7). Those laudable qualities can apparently be present, and yet God's people can quarrel and be divided over human leaders.

Clearly, verse 17 is a crucial climax and a bridge to the teaching of the next section. Observe that it was the Lord Jesus Christ who "sent" Paul to Corinth; the Greek verb used has the same root as his description of himself as an "apostle" in verse 1. But see also why he was sent—not to baptize, "but to preach the gospel". There is the focus of unity.

Observe, too, the structure of the verse: "not... but", followed by "not... lest". In that second pair of words, Paul reveals the startling choice he made. It's a great surprise to be told that "words of eloquent wisdom" could actually empty the cross of its power.

That is a real shock, because most Christians, then and now, would think that the more eloquent and the more powerful the presentation, the more successful the preaching. But Paul's astonishing point is that eloquence could, in fact, evacuate the cross of its power. It's a profound challenge to the reliance in many 21st-century churches on the star-studded, showbiz approach to public evangelization or 'worship services'. The reliance on celebrity personalities and the latest technological gimmicks might actually be emptying the cross of its power. That is a profound shock! To consider that the most entertaining, exciting and performance-oriented preachers might actually be undermining the true gospel and its proclamation should pull us up short.

But again, these observations should drive us to ask why Paul uses such startling language and such shock tactics. It is because the gospel is "the cross of Christ" (v. 17). How can the message of a crucified Saviour be proclaimed by a triumphalist preacher, whose "eloquence" draws attention to him and to his impressiveness, rather than to Jesus? Accurate observation is, once again, leading us to penetrating application.

This is also important in analysing the way in which Paul's argument now develops into a wider focus on the nature of the apostolic gospel ministry which produced the Corinthian church. Verses 17, 18 and 19 all begin with the connecting word "For", so that, from 1:18 right through to 2:5, Paul pursues and expands the main argument about the nature of the gospel.

It is striking that the contrasts of methodology in verse 17 (the "not… but" and "not… lest" patterns noted above) are echoed by a stark contrast between two groups of hearers in verse 18. Re-emphasizing that the gospel is "the word of the cross", Paul introduces the radically different reception it receives among "those who are perishing"—to whom it is folly—and "us who are being saved"—to whom it is the power of God. He is emphasizing that the real issue is not about the content of the message, which is unalterable if it is to be true to God's self-revelation, but about the attitudes of those who hear it.

Subsection 2 – 1:18-25

As we move into the next subsection, 1:18-25, I will once again need to pay close attention to the context if I am accurately and faithfully to apply its unchanging truth to our contemporary situation.

Verse 22 provides a key clue. The church in multicultural Corinth is witnessing to both Jews and Greeks, and each group has its demands, for powerful "signs" and for "wisdom", respectively. Travelling back to Corinth, then, I have to ask myself how the church has reacted to those demands, and whether this might have been the cause of the divisions Paul addressed in 1:11-12. They want their message to be received, but if its target audience of pagan unbelievers is rejecting it on the grounds of their own preconceived demands, then either the messengers are incompetent, or the message itself needs to be adapted. They are allowing the secular culture to dictate to the church its own terms about the content and methodology of their evangelism. Paul's point (made through the "For" of verse 18) is that this division is a given in all gospel proclamation. It will never be otherwise. And this is supported by the "For" introducing verse 19 and its quotation of Isaiah 29:14, in which God's own word directly confirms Paul's argument.

Whenever we meet an Old Testament reference in the New Testament, it is important not only to understand its content but also to relate it to its original context. In this case, Isaiah is rebuking the religion of

Jerusalem, which has degenerated from heart devotion to mere external formality, under the false wisdom of their religious leaders. The context is actually one of promise that God will "again do wonderful things with this people, with wonder upon wonder", but that will entail the removal of false, human-centred attitudes and values. The parallel with the wonder of the gospel, and its stark contrast with the emptiness of formal, human-centred religion, is clearly the reason for the quotation.

So working on the Old Testament context greatly contributes to the exposition of this New Testament text. Paul is not talking primarily about the philosophical theorizing of the atheistic professor at the university. Such "wisdom" is temporary and fleeting. It can never bring its adherents to God, so it is essentially foolish. But what the unbelieving world calls folly (v. 21) is God's revelation of Christ crucified, which is the only message that can save, irrespective of how it is assessed by unbelieving Jews or Greeks.

At this point in our preparation, it becomes important to begin to draw out the significance (exposition) of the paragraph. The major point is that anyone who claims an alternative "wisdom" to that which God has already revealed in the preaching of "Christ crucified" (v. 23) is doomed to be frustrated by their own folly. So why are the Corinthians so impressed by and concerned about "eloquent wisdom"? That is not going to bring anyone to God. But the fact that there is a church in Corinth and that it is composed of those who are being saved is entirely due to the proclamation of the cross of Christ, which is why Paul was sent to the city in the first place. If you want to see the power and wisdom of God, it is not in signs and human cleverness, but in your fellow believers who are being saved. The power and wisdom of God, then and now, is in Christ and the cross (vv. 23-24), wiser and stronger than every human alternative (v. 25). If this is a stumbling block and folly (v. 23), so be it; but its dynamic is that, through this message, God calls (v. 24) men and women to salvation. He determines both the content and the methodology.

As I trust this example shows, expository preaching always seeks to dig beneath the surface meaning of the text (vital though that obvious meaning is) to discover the implications and significance of what is being said. In this case, we learn that if the gospel of Christ crucified does not remain the central foundation of the Corinthian church, then ultimately it will disintegrate. The fact that it exists, as Paul writes, proves that the cross is God's power to save, although the world (v. 20) will always think it is foolishness and weakness. But without the cross there is no gospel, and without the gospel there could be no church. And so Christ crucified is central to everything; if that focus is lost, then we are back with man-made religion and merely human leaders. Baptizing (vv. 14-17a) rather than gospelling will become our raison d'être.

Once you see the context clearly, the applications to today become obvious.

USING MORE TOOLS FROM THE TOOLBOX

An 'unashamed worker' (2 Tim 2:15) knows his tools and how to use them effectively. A large part of his skill lies in selecting the right equipment for each part of the task and then utilizing it with dexterity, care and sensitivity.

There is a close analogy in this with the preacher's task in crafting a talk. So, as we move through some of the issues raised by the rest of the opening section of 1 Corinthians, I will try to identify and use some of the expositor's tools, by way of explanation. These are the kinds of tools I'd deploy on my second day of preparation, during stage 2 (exposition).

Subsections 3 and 4 – 1:26-31 and 2:1-5

We are beginning to see some of the **key words** which recur quite frequently in the text and which give us strong indicators as to the author's major concerns.

They are therefore essential ingredients of the 'melodic line', or the 'dominant tune', which governs the whole product. Here we have already noted 'wisdom' and 'power', and will soon encounter 'spiritual' and 'knowledge'. It can be helpful to trace the meaning of the original Greek text by using an expository dictionary, a lexicon or a commentary. But the precise meaning of a word in any given text is always decided ultimately by its context, which will help us to uncover the nuances at work in its specific use here.

The next two subsections, 1:26-31 and 2:1-5, now advance the argument that Paul has been building since 1:18 to its conclusion: "that your faith might not rest in the wisdom of men but in the power of God" (2:5). He wants to restore his readers' confidence in the supremacy of God's revelation in Christ and to deliver them from the snare of the fear of powerful people with their impressive, but empty, alternatives.

Another key tool is that of **sentence analysis**. This tool is particularly helpful in 1:26-31 to see where the emphasis must lie. Verses 27-29 form one long sentence, in which the main verb is repeated three times: "God chose". Identifying the main verb and its subject in any piece of New Testament prose will always direct you to the big idea. In this case, the parallelism of the structures gives Paul's statements both great clarity and authority. What God chose and why he chose it are how Paul focuses his teaching; he is deliberately contrasting God's choice with that of the world. So

God chose the foolish and weak (v. 27), the low, the despised and even the non-existent (v. 28), which are all categories of things that the world rejects. But the divine purpose is even more surprising: "to shame" the wise and the strong and "to bring to nothing" the "things that are" (vv. 27-28). This is God's deliberate policy—and verse 29 reveals his ultimate purpose: "so that no human being might boast" in his presence.

Paul has already reminded the Corinthians that not many of them measured up to the world's standards of acceptance (v. 26), but God chose them in order to destroy all boasting based on human achievement or position. So why are they now boasting about different human servants of God (1:12), dividing and quarrelling over them? They are not the source of their life. That is to be found in Christ alone, and he is the only permissible focus of pride and boasting (vv. 30-31). If they have a problem with this, then they have a problem with God, for it is God who has done the choosing. He does the calling.

So if the church at Corinth (or anywhere else) is not bursting with people who are impressive and influential in the world's eyes, it is because God has chosen the whole plan of salvation to shame and nullify human pride. It required the horrific crucifixion of his Son to rescue humanity—and if that does not shame us, what will?

As soon as a church loses its total and exclusive dependence on Christ crucified, its members will start thinking that there is something special about them. That is worldly wisdom and, in God's estimation, it is utter folly.

Once again, the parallels in application to us today are as convicting as they are obvious and unavoidable. The apostolic method is often to present profound, doctrinal truth within the setting of a practical, life-application argument, and verse 30 is an excellent example. It would be easy to pass over it without too much attention, because we are concerned to follow the main flow of the argument. But it presents the important counterbalance of positive teaching to all the Corinthian error that the apostle has been exposing.

Since all our preaching is designed to proclaim Christ, the heart of all Scripture, the wise expositor will want to give time to verse 30, so as to *State*, *Explain* and *Apply* what it means that Christ, the source of our life, is made our wisdom, righteousness, sanctification and redemption. In this way, as the glories of Christ are exhibited, the tawdry nature of human pride and its attendant divisions and quarrels are exposed for the folly that they are. We must ensure that Christ is uplifted and that the passage enlarges our understanding of who he is and what he has accomplished, so that the Corinthian failures are eclipsed by his majestic glory. We do not want our hearers to go away overwhelmed by the mistakes of the church, but rejoicing in the glory of the Lord.

The final clinching ingredient of Paul's argument

is in 2:1-5, where he uses himself and his ministry at Corinth as the evidence and illustration of the spiritual principles he has been teaching.

Again, it is important to identify the progression of the structure. Beginning by reminding his readers that his own ministry was not "with lofty speech or wisdom" (v. 1), he explains his reasons in a sequence which flows from verse 2 to verse 5, introduced again by the connective "For". The main verb is "I decided"—this was his deliberate choice and intention—and from this flows the message (v. 2), the condition of the messenger (vv. 3-4a), and the outcome of this strategy (vv. 4b-5). The fact that Paul came in "weakness and in fear and much trembling" made it abundantly clear that the ability to transform lives lay in the message, not the messenger; in the Spirit's power, not in words of wisdom (v. 4).

In teaching material like this, we will want to draw out the surprises it entails, so as to maximize its impact on us. For example, it is striking that you can have a weak, fearful, trembling preacher, but at the same time the demonstration of the Spirit's power. Most of us don't readily believe that today. But the evidence is that the Spirit produces faith (v. 5). People should not go away saying, "What a marvellous communicator!" when they've heard your preaching, but rather should go away putting their faith in Jesus as a wonderful rescuer. Note too that the word of the cross and the power of the Spirit always belong together, and that divine power is always most evident in human weakness.

This should be a great encouragement to us as we think about how we teach strong-meat passages like this to a contemporary audience. The applications need to be drawn out with clarity and courage, because the necessary recalibrations will not always be well received.

First, we must apply its teaching to our own lives. Where are we putting our confidence as we seek to teach the Bible? What authority do we look to and minister under? The church is always tempted to look to human authorities, rather than the word of the cross. There are plenty of substitutes on offer—scholarship, tradition, institutional rules and regulations, experience, and sacramentalism, to name just a few. We may, of course, want to affirm that we are gospel people ("I follow Christ"; 1:12), but it is all too easy to allow that focus to become blurred, or even to move away from it. We can become more committed to the church than to Christ, its head. We can love gospel work more than we love the Lord of the gospel. We can be more concerned for the growth and success of our particular tribe than for the glory of God. These are challenges that contemporary evangelicalism needs to hear.

At this point, you may be feeling, "But who am I to speak to my fellow Christians in this way?" I hope you are, both because it means that you are being kept humble and also because you will apply corrective passages with love and with sensitivity. Paul himself would later entreat the Corinthians "by the meekness and gentleness of Christ" (2 Cor 10:1), so we must seek to follow in his steps. Of course, we have no right in and of ourselves to set ourselves up to correct our fellow believers. Controlling personalities, who are always laying down the law to others and telling them what they should be doing, do not commend the gospel of grace.

And yet, if the Bible says it, the church needs to hear it. If the church doesn't hear what may seem to be unpalatable from its preachers and teachers, then the danger is that it will not hear it at all. The issues will not be addressed or dealt with. The wrong priorities and emphases will predominate unchecked, and the vitality of the whole body will gradually drain away. The expositor's calling is to be faithful, not popular.

Subsection 5 – 2:6-16

One of the most effective tools at the teacher's disposal is that of **contrast**. We seem to learn well by examining opposites: not this, but that. And we often understand the positives more clearly when we examine the other side of the coin and learn from the negatives. In fact, biblically, teaching the negatives is one of the most effective ways of underlining the positive truth.

The next section, 2:6-16, provides an informative example of Paul's method, which reminds us that Scripture not only tells us *what to teach* but also *how to teach it*.

The end of 2:4 introduced us for the first time in the letter to the powerful Spirit, whose ministry now begins to become the central focus. We have already seen the contrast between the world's wisdom and the wisdom of God, but this is now unpacked much more extensively in a series of developed contrasts between the human and the divine.

One way of teaching the passage, then, could be to list the contrasting characteristics of these alternative forms of "wisdom". Giving a talk some structure like this can often reinforce its message to our hearers.

There seem to be five contrasts that Paul wants to highlight, which he does by beginning with the weakness and inadequacy of the human before moving on to the superiority of the divine:

- » In verses 6-7, human wisdom is temporal and transient. By contrast, divine wisdom is revealed by God and is eternal.
- » In verses 8-10, human wisdom is ignorant of God and his salvation plan through the cross, for if people had understood, they would not have crucified the Lord of glory. By contrast, all the eternal blessings of divine wisdom have been revealed to God's people by his Spirit, through the gospel.
- » In verses 11-12, human wisdom can never rise above human comprehension. By contrast, divine wisdom is a revelation of the mind and heart of God.

- » In verse 13, Paul pursues the massive difference he has highlighted in verses 11-12 and shows that human wisdom is always confined to human categories. By contrast, divine wisdom communicates to the spirit of human beings by the Spirit of God.
- » In verses 14-16, human wisdom, because it has no divine illumination, is unable to come to a right judgement about spiritual matters. By contrast, divine wisdom is not subject to human judgements, because through it the mind of God is being revealed to his people.

After this extensive exercise of comparison and contrast, we can see why Paul began the section as he did in verse 6, saying that spiritual wisdom is the possession of the "mature": the mature are those who, by definition, are taught by the Spirit of God.

It has been said that the purpose of preaching is "to disturb the comfortable and then to comfort the disturbed". This passage certainly seems to have that intention, as an implicit question runs through all the contrasts: which side of the divide you are on? The answer to this question is the difference between growing in spiritual maturity and suffering arrested development, which the next verse (3:1) describes as being "people of the flesh… infants in Christ". The Corinthians were in danger of consigning themselves to perpetual spiritual immaturity through their wrong priorities, although they were "enriched in him in all speech and all knowledge" and "not lacking in any gift" (1:5, 7). Those, however, were not the marks of spiritual maturity in the gospel, which were evidenced in the self-sacrificing love of the cross.

The danger and challenge for the church is that the world constantly puts forward its own solutions to the problems which only the gospel can solve. Buying into that human wisdom will always lead to compromise and a loss of Christian distinctiveness, because it is only the gospel that can change our human lives fundamentally.

We should be praying that our teaching of this passage will give us and our hearers renewed confidence in the gospel and dependence on the Spirit's power, so that we too may see God's call at work in saving many individuals and transforming society.

HOW THE TEXT DRIVES THE TALK

The rest of the opening section of 1 Corinthians (chapters 1-4) can be divided into three major parts: 3:1-15, 3:16-4:7 and 4:8-21. It is not our purpose here to cover the content in any great detail.[3] But I want to use these passages to illustrate what it means to have the text in the driving seat as we move through the preparation process from the work of exposition to the structure and strategy of the talk or teaching.

Subsection 6 – 3:1-15

At the start of chapter 3, Paul returns to the contentious issues that were dividing the church into a number of camps, each following a particular leader. First, he diagnoses the cause of this, which he identifies as spiritual immaturity—what he calls "being merely

---

3 I have tried to do that in my book *Let's Study 1 Corinthians*, Banner of Truth Trust, 2004.

human" (v. 4b). This builds on the contrast between the human and divine which we saw expounded in chapter 2. It is human behaviour to elevate favoured leaders against others, but the remedy is to realize that in the life of the church a totally different set of values and priorities must predominate, according to the "secret and hidden wisdom of God" (2:7).

The Corinthians should not think of Paul or Apollos (or anyone else) as leaders to be followed, but simply as "servants through whom you believed" (3:5). Paul and Apollos had different tasks (planting and watering, respectively), but the growth was totally dependent on God alone, and "each will receive his wages according to his labour" (v. 8). That wage, or "reward" (v. 14b), is firmly fixed in the future when "the Day"—presumably the day of Christ and of the judgement—will reveal the quality of each servant's work (v. 13). There is only one foundation, which is Jesus Christ, and all building on that foundation needs to be done with the finest quality materials and with diligent skill. The work of the "servant" is not done to acquire an adoring fan club, all tweeting their 'likes', but to be tested by Christ and to seek his approval, as it is his temple, the church, that is under construction.

The passage clearly presents us with the requirement of recognizing a totally different set of criteria for evaluating Christian leadership, which is actually self-giving service. So a talk based on this passage should reflect that priority. Everything that lasts in the growth of the church is given by God. Everything will ultimately be tested by God, according to "what sort of work each one has done" (v. 13b). In this scenario, human judgements are irrelevant. What matters is the wisdom from above, taught by the Spirit, which is the mind of Christ (2:12-16).

Subsection 7 – 3:16-4:7

The next section (3:16-4:7) is introduced by a question which is more than rhetorical, and which is expressed by a formula to be used ten times in the letter: "Do you not know…?" It is not just an expression of frustration, though clearly there is some element of impatience as he writes to a church "enriched… in all knowledge" (1:5). But this seems to be part of the problem. Later, in 8:1, Paul quotes what seems to be the Corinthians' affirmation, "all of us possess knowledge". He does this, however, to devastating effect as he continues, "This 'knowledge' puffs up, but love builds up". If they really are so advanced in knowledge, surely there are basic things they should be aware of and living by; but they seem to have forgotten or ignored these things.

This short example adds another tool to our toolbox: looking for **repetition of phrases, vocabulary and ideas** is an important discipline in enabling us to keep interpreting the passage currently under the microscope in the context of the whole book and its 'melodic line'.

Verses 18-23 illustrate the same principle by use of

the repeated formula, "Let no-one…", which divides the paragraph into two: "Let no-one deceive himself" (vv. 18-20) and "let no-one boast in men" (vv. 21-23). The two are, of course, closely interconnected—the deceit leads to the boasting, so the boasting is evidence of being deceived.

What we're seeing at work here is one of the great principles of expository preaching: pursue the logic of the text, and the talk you are to give almost begins to write itself! The expositor's task is not to cleverly develop a structure that he or she can then impose on the text; it is to observe and utilize the structure provided by the text itself.

In this passage, we've observed that the deception is thinking that Christians have the option to embrace the world's wisdom. That is utter folly, as two Old Testament quotes (from Job 5:13 and Psalm 94:11) indicate, stressing the superiority and eternality of divine wisdom. So what is there to boast about in anything human? Everything of ultimate value comes from God, through Christ, and is freely given for the benefit of his people, "for all things are yours" (v. 21).

Notice how the clear negative instructions are expounded by the reasons for them, and how these are all grounded in the supremacy of God over everything he has made. His being is infinite and of an entirely different quality from his creation. If the text drives the talk, this must be a major take-home benefit of the passage—that our vision of God is immeasurably expanded, and our image of ourselves equivalently shrunk.

These verses can be summarized and taught in terms of the perils that Paul sees the Corinthian church is facing, but of which they seem to have been largely oblivious. They are in danger of:

- » destroying the church, God's holy temple, through their immature divisions (vv. 16-17)
- » deceiving themselves by rejecting God's wisdom in favour of merely human ideas (vv. 18-20)
- » glorifying or boasting about men, when everything they have is totally dependent on God (vv. 21-23).

Actually, these three perils sum up Paul's concerns in the first three chapters. Many commentators place the emphasis on the way that internal wrangling will tear a church apart. But Gordon Fee suggests that destroying God's temple may mean that, if these issues are not addressed, they will destroy the church's ability to function as a viable alternative to the pagan temples which proliferated in Corinth.[4] A major purpose of God's temple (the believers) was to expose the emptiness of man-made religion and human philosophy by demonstrating the power of Christ crucified to produce a community of selfless love and service, reflecting his own divine priorities. The authenticity of the gospel is

---

4 GD Fee, *The First Epistle to the Corinthians*, rev. edn, New International Commentary on the New Testament, Eerdmans, 2014.

proved by the quality of life-change that it produces, both then and now.

Insights like these are a powerful confirmation of the unrivalled value of consecutive exposition of the Scriptures, section by section, book by book, as the regular teaching program of every local church. After all, this is how God has given us his revelation—in whole books, written to specific situations with specific purposes. Understanding the flow of the argument greatly helps us to work with the text as we seek to connect its unchanging truth to our own contemporary circumstances.

As we prepare our teaching, we must always be looking for ways in which we can enable the Bible's truth to cross the bridge from the original context to our own, with clarity and penetration. Chapter 4 offers a further illustration of this principle.

In chapter 4, Paul is expounding the perils into which the Corinthians are drifting. In the first seven verses, the emphasis moves from exhortation ("Let no-one…") to explanation. So our teaching of this section must reflect that shift. The focus now is on why they were going wrong and how right thinking will correct those errors.

Paul returns to the way in which they regarded him and the other 'leaders' whom the different factions favoured. He begins with the positive. What is the right evaluation of those whom God has used to plant and nurture the church, such as himself and

Apollos? Not overlords, but "servants" and "stewards" (v. 1), both of which positions are entirely dependent on God's provision. Christ is the master, and the mysteries of God are the resources given. That is why the standard of judgement is not human success, but godly faithfulness (v. 2).

Observing the flow of logic, we see that Paul now begins to list what is wrong in Corinth (vv. 3-5). They are judging by the wrong standards, in the wrong court, and at the wrong time. The key concept is stated at the heart of the paragraph at the end of verse 4. "It is the Lord who judges". God's standard is trustworthiness and his judgement is infallible. But that awaits his return, and only then will the inner motivations of people's hearts be revealed. In the meantime, the Corinthians' attitude is actually usurping God's authority.

Verses 6-7, then, are clearly a conclusion to the section by which Paul puts his finger on the heart attitude that lies behind their presumptuous judgements. "All these things" (v. 6) probably refers us back to the contents of the first three chapters, from which they need to learn "not to go beyond what is written". Scripture is where God's mind is revealed, so to introduce their own, unbiblical standards of judgement is to err, to go further than they should. And the motivation to do so is pride, described as being "puffed up" (v. 6). They seem to have forgotten that every Christian is always totally dependent on God's grace; literally every good thing we have is the gift of God. It has been received, so there is nothing to boast about. But where grace is forgotten, pride asserts itself and produces the wrong judges, with the wrong standards, in the wrong court, at the wrong time. As we have already seen, "Let the one who boasts, boast in the Lord" (1:31).

So, how might all these observations work in terms of our preparation? A theme sentence would perhaps be: "The great perils by which a living church can be destroyed." This would lead to an *aim sentence* like this: "My hearers (and I) will recognize and then eliminate the dangers of divisions and pride in a local church, which can so easily neutralize an effective gospel witness."

The main points of the talk would then be developed around the marker posts in the text, which we have already identified. Because the passage is so clearly corrective, you might decide to express them as negative imperatives, which add urgency and demand, and which are supported by the explanations all the way through the section. "Don't destroy the church." "Don't deceive yourselves." "Don't glorify men."

The conclusion could then underline that human pride causes such errors, and call the hearers to be faithful servants of Christ.

Subsection 8 – 4:8-21

The section concludes with a passage of great emotional intensity, in which Paul reveals what being a servant of Christ has cost him, in direct contrast to the values which the Corinthians have adopted (4:8-13). This is followed by a moving personal appeal to imitate their "father in Christ Jesus through the gospel" (v. 15), to put aside their foolish and destructive talk, bred by their arrogance, and to embrace again the true power inherent only in God's kingly rule (vv. 14-21).

The autobiographical section begins with stark contrasts between the triumphalist self-satisfaction of the Corinthians, expressed ironically in verse 8 ("Already you have all you want!"), and ends with a crescendo of sufferings for Christ, culminating in Paul's testimony, "We have become, and are still, like the scum of the world, the refuse of all things" (v. 13).

The "you"/"we" contrast is powerfully sustained throughout, and the challenge is renewed again and again. Will the readers stand with the rejected apostle of the rejected Saviour, for Christ's sake and the gospel's (v. 10)? Or will they side with the aspirations of arrogance, to become rich, to reign as kings (v. 8)?

The final appeal is consciously warm, based on the relationship Paul has with his "beloved children" (v. 14) as their "father… through the gospel". Timothy is instanced as a "beloved and faithful child in the Lord" (v. 17), which is what Paul longs for the Corinthians to become, so that when he visits it may be in love and gentleness, not with a rod of discipline (v. 21).

The choice is clearly presented: only the power of the gospel of Christ crucified could keep the apostles labouring, blessing, enduring and entreating

(vv. 12-13), but that is the greatness of the power of God's kingdom (v. 20). In comparison, the arrogant "talk" of the divisive factions of the church in Corinth is a pathetic travesty of the true gospel and its transformative wisdom and power.

This last section reminds us that, in the books of Acts, one of the verbs most frequently used to describe the nature of apostolic ministry is "persuade". Here we see Paul at his persuasive best. He doesn't pull his punches, but he is motivated by a sacrificial love which wants to produce the best responses in the lives of those whom he serves in Christ's name.

However we might structure our exposition of this concluding section, it will fail accurately to represent the text's intention if it does not seek to be equally persuasive. Expository preaching is sometimes unfairly caricatured as "all head and no heart", but there is a real point that is being made. In our desire to be accurate and correct, we can sometimes squeeze the life out of the passage and reduce its emotional intensity to formal statements.

One of the reasons to pay attention to the way in which the different genres of biblical writing appeal to different aspects of the whole person (mind, heart, affections, will) is that it prevents the preacher from putting every text through the same mincing machine and coming out with a predictable set of theological propositions. We must not be afraid of emotional content in our teaching, since there is so much of it in the Bible text itself, as here in this passage. What we need to reject is emotionalism, by which I mean the preacher making a deliberate attempt to play on the emotions of the hearers by seeking to engineer a response through his or her own inventive brilliance. Such 'pulpiteering' may seem to produce a powerful immediate effect, but that may well be as fleeting as the emotion itself, because that is all it is. It is only the word of the Lord that remains forever; this eternal word must form the content of all our teaching if it is to have any lasting impact in time and for eternity.

TOOLS FROM THE UNASHAMED WORKER'S TOOLBOX

Throughout our study of the first section of Paul's letter, I have mentioned and illustrated a number of tools that the preacher might apply from his or her toolbox, depending on the nature and content of the passage for the Bible talk. Here is an expanded list of some of the tools I have accumulated and used over the years. I have deliberately kept my list and the explanation of each item brief, so that you can get a sense of how each tool might help you without feeling burdened by a long, strict set of rules. So long as these tools help you to grapple with the text of Scripture on its own terms, they can be refined to suit your style and your situation. You should use this list as a reference to consider which tools might best serve you in working through a particular passage. Over time, you may also develop your own tools which you can add to the list.[5]

Topping and tailing: Pay close attention to the start and finish of the passage, as this will often open up the central ideas of the text.

Key words: Look for repetition, and let the context show you how repeated words are used and what they mean.

Connecting words: These words (e.g. therefore, for, because, so that, and, but) help you to establish the flow of thought in the passage and relate the ideas to one another.

Analyse sentences: Pay special attention to the main verbs and their tenses (e.g. past, present, future). This helps you to keep the main thing the main thing.

Note the surprises: When something seems odd to you—when you wouldn't have said that, or you wouldn't have said it at that point in the passage—stop and try to work out why the author has said it. How does he correct your wrong or inadequate thinking?

Teach the positives through the negatives: We often understand something better by seeing its opposite, or what it is not.

---

5   For an expanded list of tools, I recommend my three-module series *Equipped to Preach the Word*, available for free download on the Proclamation Trust website. proctrust.org.uk/equipped

Keep asking why: Why this, why here, and why in these words? This helps us to dig deeper into the text, and not to be content with surface meanings only.

Compare Scripture with Scripture: How is this text echoed, expanded or fulfilled elsewhere in the Bible? In particular, how does this text point us to Christ? Use the principle of cumulative revelation, where the later texts interpret the earlier.

Cut with the grain of the wood: Work with the way the author has put the book or passage together. Follow its major themes in your passage.

Travel back to Corinth (before you try to bring Corinthians into the present day): Work out what the text meant to the original recipients before bringing its message to us now.

Check your vocabulary: Consider the language you plan to use in your talk. Is it understandable and contemporary? Have you avoided abstract nouns and past tenses? Are your main points expressed as teaching points, rather than being simply descriptive?

In narratives, look for the turning point: This is where the 'problem' in the text starts to be solved, and it will usually yield the main teaching point.

In prophecy, look for three points of reference: the *original context*, the *fulfilment in Christ*, and the *future fulfilment in eternity*. What did this prophecy mean to its original hearers back then? What difference does the coming of Jesus make? What is the prophecy's future, eternal significance?

In poetry, look for parallelism: This is a favourite poetic device of many authors of biblical poetry. Look carefully at the two parts of the verse. If parallelism has been used, what does it achieve? For example, does it provide reinforcement or intensity? Emphasis or explanation? Comparison or contrast?

TEN 'COMMANDMENTS' FOR PREACHING

It is said that if it takes several hours to prepare a Bible talk, it takes a lifetime to prepare the preacher. At first that may sound daunting, an impossible goal. But in fact it is very encouraging, because it means that teaching the Bible well is an ongoing challenge—something at which we can (and must) make constant progress.

In that sense, the dynamic is exactly the same as that of living the Christian life, deepening in spiritual maturity and growing in godliness. Paul put it this way: "Not that I have already obtained this or am already perfect, but I press on to make it my own, because Christ Jesus has made me his own" (Phil 3:12). What should characterize every disciple applies in a special sense to every teacher of God's word.

So, what do we need to remember? What do we need to work out as we move from text to teaching? Let me suggest ten 'commandments'.

1. The text must *always* be in the driver's seat

It determines the content, the mood, and even the structure of the teaching. We need to immerse our own minds and hearts in the text and ensure that it ministers to the teacher before an attempt is made to pass it on to others.

2. Work out the *theme sentence* for the talk

This will help you to keep the main thing the main thing, and will enable you to present your material in a coherent and unified way. Ask yourself: What *must* I preach from this text if I am to be faithful to both its divine author and his human mouthpiece?

3. Make sure that you establish equal clarity about the *aim sentence* for the teaching you are preparing

What was your text's purpose in its original context for those first hearers or readers? How does that relate to the situation and the needs of those whom you will be teaching? What are you going to pray that God will be pleased to accomplish through this talk or study? Why are you giving this talk? Get your aim clear. Focus your target.

4. Remember that you are not writing an essay, but speaking to real people in all of life's ups and downs

They are people with all sorts of aspirations, hopes, fears, disappointments, perplexities, doubts, and so on. They are whole people; they have *minds* that need to be informed, *hearts* that need to be warmed and softened, and *wills* that need to be energized and empowered.

Try to make sure that you make strong and meaningful connections from the text to your hearers, whatever their current situation.

5. Take care to explain the major content of the text

This teaching is the spiritual nourishment for building up the body of Christ, both individually and corporately. The Bible never commands us to do anything without first explaining why and how, which is another way of saying that it always addresses the whole person—mind, heart and will. To put it another way, the imperatives (what we must do) always flow from the indicatives (what God has done). There can be no commands without the promises, no required action without the instruction. Make sure you teach both.

6. Help your hearers to journey with you by providing a clear road map, or agenda, of where you intend to go

Every talk needs to be a logical progression from where the text is to where our hearers are. That is why the main points of the talk need to be articulated as clearly and memorably as possible. They serve as signposts on the path. Try to make the way you state the point teach the point. Don't be content with merely descriptive headings, but try to make them didactic—points that teach. This will give the talk its edge.

7. Preaching has been described as "truth through personality"

The truth of God's revelation is unchanging, but every teacher will present it in their own unique way. No-one else will do it like you, so don't you try to do it like someone else, however much of a hero they may be to you. Develop your own unique style and voice. Don't allow your personal style to override the message of the text, but ask God to use your personality to teach his truth, so that what you present is authentic and real.

8. Make sure your applications can all be justified by reference to the Bible text

Ensure your applications are not being driven by your current obsessions, or those of your 'tribe' or 'in group'. Many preachers are adept at bolting on 'ought to' applications from their general theological framework, but these are often a substitute for hard work and careful reflection. We probably ought to pray more, read the Bible more, give more, serve more, and so on. But is that what *this* passage is saying? If not, your generic application will lack the power and conviction that come when Bible applications are made of Bible truth.

9. Remember that you don't have to be clever, but faithful, which is not the same as being boring

There can be no excuse for being dull. But our priority is not to find the smartest, most startling headings, or the most dramatic or humorous illustrations. Our first responsibility is always to explain the text. Often preachers state a point, then jump immediately into an illustration, and then on to an application based on the illustration, so that the explanation of meaning and significance becomes obscured. Hearers remember the illustration, but do they remember what the illustration was intended to teach?

10. Pray, pray, and pray!

"Unless the LORD builds the house, those who build it labour in vain" (Ps 127:1). The Bible constantly reminds us of this principle. Jesus told his disciples, "Apart from me you can do nothing" (John 15:5). Or, as Paul reminded the Corinthians, it is "only God who gives the growth" (1 Cor 3:7).

Pray when you begin your preparation, for the Holy Spirit's gracious illumination of the word he has inspired.

Pray as you write your notes, for God-given accuracy, effectiveness, structure and vocabulary.

Pray before you preach or teach, pray even as you are speaking, and pray afterwards, for lasting fruit.

Pray all the way through the process, for discernment, wisdom, clarity and obedience.

Pray, as the old prayer puts it, that God's word may be our rule, his Holy Spirit our guide, and his greater glory our supreme concern.

APPENDIX: TEMPLATE FOR PREPARING A BIBLE TALK

Passage: _____ Date: _____

Occasion: _____

Pray, pray, and pray again!
Read, read, and read again!

Exegesis

What are the main ideas within the text?

How do the main ideas relate to each other?

Plot out the flow of thought in the passage.

How does this passage relate to its immediate context (what comes before and after it), to the book of which it is a part, and to the developing revelation in the whole Bible?

Express its major teaching content in the form of a theme sentence.

Exposition

What is the main significance of the passage?

Why do you think the author included it here? What is its controlling purpose?

How does it point us to Jesus Christ?

How does its transformational purpose translate to us in our contemporary context?

Express the main purpose of your talk in an aim sentence.

Structure

What will be the main points as you teach the passage, and how will you express them?

What applications will you feature, and where in the text do they come from?

Which illustrations will you use, and for what purpose?

How will you conclude the talk?

Plan an introduction that will serve the aim of the talk and engage the hearers.

matthiasmedia

Matthias Media is an evangelical publishing ministry that seeks to persuade all Christians of the truth of God's purposes in Jesus Christ as revealed in the Bible, and equip them with high-quality resources, so that by the work of the Holy Spirit they will:

- abandon their lives to the honour and service of Christ in daily holiness and decision-making
- pray constantly in Christ's name for the fruitfulness and growth of his gospel
- speak the Bible's life-changing word whenever and however they can—in the home, in the world and in the fellowship of his people.

Our wide range of resources includes Bible studies, books, training courses, tracts and children's material. To find out more, and to access samples and free downloads, visit our website:

www.matthiasmedia.com

How to buy our resources

1. Direct from us over the internet:
   - in the US: www.matthiasmedia.com
   - in Australia: www.matthiasmedia.com.au

2. Direct from us by phone: please visit our website for current phone contact information.

3. Through a range of outlets in various parts of the world. Visit **www.matthiasmedia.com/contact** for details about recommended retailers in your part of the world.

4. Trade enquiries can be addressed to:
   - in the US and Canada: sales@matthiasmedia.com
   - in Australia and the rest of the world: sales@matthiasmedia.com.au

Register at our website for our **free** regular email update to receive information about the latest new resources, **exclusive special offers**, and free articles to help you grow in your Christian life and ministry.

How to Read the Bible Better

Richard Chin

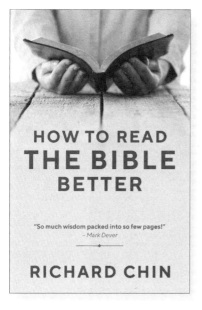

Excited? Daunted? Curious?

How do you feel about the Bible?

No matter how you feel about the world's bestselling book, we can all use a guiding hand to help us make the most of our Bible reading. In this short, readable book, pastor and preacher Richard Chin offers you a step-by-step guide to better Bible reading: how to make sense of the Scriptures, how to avoid the most common pitfalls, and how to let God's word shape your life.

FOR MORE INFORMATION OR TO ORDER CONTACT:

Matthias Media
Email: sales@matthiasmedia.com.au
www.matthiasmedia.com.au

Matthias Media (USA)
Email: sales@matthiasmedia.com
www.matthiasmedia.com

Saving Eutychus
Gary Millar and Phil Campbell

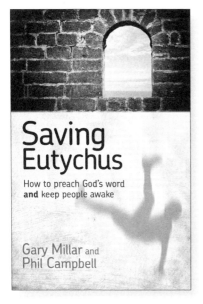

Poor Eutychus might have tumbled off his perch in Acts 20, but it's humbling to notice that what took Paul many hours of preaching to achieve—near-fatal napping in one of his listeners—takes most preachers only a few minutes on a Sunday.

Saving Eutychus will help you save your listeners from such a fate. Written by an Aussie and an Irishman with very different styles who share a passion for preaching the gospel of Jesus Christ, *Saving Eutychus* delivers fresh, honest, faithful and practical insights into preaching the whole word of God, Sunday by Sunday, without being dull. This book is a practical distillation of decades of thinking, writing, preaching, failing, humbly praying and seeing God at work, and it's an invaluable tool for honing your own gifts to become the best preacher you can be.

Includes sermons and mutual critique from each author, a sermon critique sheet, and practical tips and helpful diagrams.

FOR MORE INFORMATION OR TO ORDER CONTACT:

Matthias Media
Email: sales@matthiasmedia.com.au
www.matthiasmedia.com.au

Matthias Media (USA)
Email: sales@matthiasmedia.com
www.matthiasmedia.com

Being a Small Group Leader
Richard Sweatman

What makes someone a good small group leader?

A comprehensive knowledge of the Bible? Wisdom that rivals Solomon's? Exceptional people skills? Or is willingness and availability enough?

Richard Sweatman uses the Bible and his years of small group ministry experience to highlight five vital areas in which we need to keep growing as Christian leaders: knowledge of God, character, teaching ability, encouragement of others, and team leadership.

Whether you've been leading a small group for days or decades, you'll find warm encouragement to identify areas in which you can improve, and you'll be challenged and helped to make realistic plans for doing so.

This book is also a useful resource for pastors to work through in talking with those who might take up this valuable ministry in the future.

FOR MORE INFORMATION OR TO ORDER CONTACT:

Matthias Media
Email: sales@matthiasmedia.com.au
www.matthiasmedia.com.au

Matthias Media (USA)
Email: sales@matthiasmedia.com
www.matthiasmedia.com

The Archer and the Arrow
Phillip Jensen and Paul Grimmond

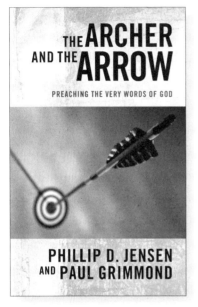

This book is about a sentence 40 years in the making. The sentence is Phillip Jensen's summary of the preacher's mission, gained from a lifetime of biblical reflection and practice:

> **My aim is to preach the gospel by prayerfully expounding the Bible to the people God has given me to love.**

Join Phillip Jensen and Paul Grimmond as they explore each phrase in this carefully wrought statement, and show not only why faithful, powerful, biblical preaching is so important, but how to go about it.

FOR MORE INFORMATION OR TO ORDER CONTACT:

Matthias Media
Email: sales@matthiasmedia.com.au
www.matthiasmedia.com.au

Matthias Media (USA)
Email: sales@matthiasmedia.com
www.matthiasmedia.com

Know and Tell the Gospel
John Chapman

For most believers, clearly sharing the Christian gospel with someone is more of a dream than a reality. We feel inadequate and reluctant—but we absolutely want to see our friends come to know Jesus.

Filled with heart and humour, *Know and Tell the Gospel* deals with all the questions that quickly come to mind:

- Just what is the gospel anyway?
- Is it my job to explain it to people?
- What is God's role and what is mine?
- Where does church fit in?
- Why is evangelism so often hard?
- How can we train ourselves and others to be involved?

Every Christian keen to take the gospel to our lost world must read this encouragement from John Chapman, a man who had more than 50 years of experience with evangelism and Bible teaching.

FOR MORE INFORMATION OR TO ORDER CONTACT:

Matthias Media
Email: sales@matthiasmedia.com.au
www.matthiasmedia.com.au

Matthias Media (USA)
Email: sales@matthiasmedia.com
www.matthiasmedia.com